IMAGES
*of America*

# SAC COUNTY

F.C. Hoyt was a photographer who produced thousands of real-photo postcards with Sac City and Sac County images. His efforts and business acumen helped preserve Sac County history. The racks of postcards are visible through the door of his store that specialized in photographs, sewing machines, sporting goods, and Indian motorcycles. Hoyt loved to travel around Sac City in his sporty car. (Author's collection.)

ON THE COVER: A quintet of young spectators poses in front of the 1908 Chautauqua pavilion in Sac City. The Chautauqua movement brought traveling shows to many communities. The success of the two-week programs prompted Sac City residents to erect a permanent auditorium to set their community apart from other towns that used a large tent for their shows. The tent-like building, listed in the National Register of Historic Places, still stands as a monument to the national movement that helped shape rural culture. (Author's collection.)

IMAGES
*of America*

# SAC COUNTY

Bruce Perry

ARCADIA
PUBLISHING

Published by Arcadia Publishing
Charleston, South Carolina

Printed in the United States of America

Library of Congress Control Number: 2019956574

For all general information, please contact Arcadia Publishing:
Telephone 843-853-2070
Fax 843-853-0044
E-mail sales@arcadiapublishing.com
For customer service and orders:
Toll-Free 1-888-313-2665

Visit us on the Internet at www.arcadiapublishing.com

*This book is dedicated to my parents, Hubert and Loraine (Manly) Perry, whose love of storytelling and prodigious memory for detail instilled my love of local history. Without their inspiration, this snapshot of Sac County would not be possible.*

# CONTENTS

# ACKNOWLEDGMENTS

Two photographers are responsible for many of the historical images in this collection. Hoyt Photography in Sac City produced more than 10,000 real-photo postcards (RPPCs) of Sac City and the surrounding area. Traver Photography in Odebolt captured many scenes with his lens. Thanks in large part to their efforts, a glimpse into Sac County's past can become a snapshot of the area between 1890 and 1930.

All images come from the author's personal collection of vintage RPPCs and photographs.

# INTRODUCTION

Sac County, located in the northwest quadrant of Iowa, offers a wide array of agricultural resources, beautiful topography, and cultural activities for the more than 10,000 residents who inhabit the 578 square miles within the county borders. Prior to becoming a county in 1851, the area was home to the Fox and Sauk (Sac) Native Americans, after whom the county was named.

The county's rich agricultural soil was, in large part, due to glacial deposits. The Wisconsin glacier covered the eastern part of the county, creating the natural drainage divide that bisects the county and sends water either to the Missouri or Mississippi Rivers. The glacier also created Black Hawk Lake, the southernmost glacial lake in Iowa. The allure of farming was a major attraction for settlers who began to come to Sac County in the 1850s. Land prices of $3 an acre or less made settling the area affordable. Traveling by oxcart was most common for settlers. Building a residence on the property was a requirement for new property owners. D. Carr Early, one of Sac County's first residents, walked 90 miles to register claims for himself and a friend while the friend built a house that straddled the border of the adjacent properties the two men claimed.

This hardy stock of residents spread the word that Sac County was a vibrant land of opportunity. By 1860, a total of 246 people called Sac County home. Ten years later, the population had grown to 1,411. The 1900 Census showed the county population burgeoning to 17,639 residents.

Sac City was named the county seat in 1856 and has been home to three courthouses in addition to an early log structure that served as the first seat of government. As the population increased, numerous towns sprang up throughout the county.

Sac City, the oldest community in the county, was founded in 1855. Grant City, which is no longer incorporated, was laid out in 1863. Odebolt was platted in 1877 after the Chicago & Northwest Railway extended to that point. Platted in 1877, Wall Lake took its name from the nearby Wall Lake (now known as Black Hawk Lake). Schaller, named after prominent Civil War veteran Phil Schaller who lived in Sac City, was founded in 1879 as a railroad town. James Fletcher built a railroad station in 1880 and laid out the town of Fletcher; in 1887, the town was incorporated and changed its name to Lake View to honor the beautiful vista of what is now called Black Hawk Lake. The town of Early incorporated in 1883 and was named after D. Carr Early, a prominent Sac City resident and real estate developer. Auburn, platted in 1888, was named after Auburn, New York. Nemaha, platted in 1899, grew because of the railroad. Lytton, which includes parts of Sac and Calhoun Counties, was established in 1899 and named after English author Edward Bulwer-Lytton.

One of the first steps to transform the virgin prairie into arable farmland was to survey the land and create a layout for property lines. John F. Duncombe of Fort Dodge helped plat the county, which was divided into square mile sections with occasional correction lines to account for the earth's curvature. Sac City began to develop along the stagecoach line between Fort Dodge and Sergeant Bluff. The town, enveloped in the curvature of the North Raccoon River, became a favorite stopping place for travelers. As more residents moved to the county and rural residents needed nearby places to shop and a market for crops, other communities began to flourish.

Many who purchased land worked tirelessly to find the most effective ways to produce abundant crops and effective farming operations. Early crop rotation practices, designed to promote improved yields, included planting corn, hay, oats, and pasture coverings. The search for crop diversity lead many to plant popcorn, which is ideally suited to the county's soil and growing conditions. Cracker Jacks, Jiffy Time, Snappy, and Noble popcorn companies developed, in large part, because of the popcorn grown in the area. In later years, soybeans became a staple crop for the county. Landowners worked with the land grant university in Ames (now Iowa State University) to develop better seed stock and plant varieties to match growing conditions. Livestock producers utilized selective breeding to create the best possible herds of cattle, sheep, horses, poultry, and swine. Two large landholdings near Odebolt, the Adams Ranch and Cook Ranch, known as bonanza farms, explored new purchasing, marketing, and management methods to maximize profits. These large farming operations laid much of the groundwork for modern agricultural practices that have enabled Iowa to become a leader in world crop production.

Sac County farms have not only helped feed the world, but have also provided significant financial resources for residents to construct beautiful communities, attract industry and commerce, develop rich cultural and artistic traditions, and support infrastructure to connect the various communities to each other and the surrounding area.

As communities began to grow, local businesspersons erected beautiful stores and homes. Sac County is home to many wonderful examples of architecture. Queen Anne homes, Second Empire structures, buildings designed by noted architects, and striking public buildings continue to enrich the area. Churches and schools became focal points for each community. Each community gradually acquired its own character. Auburn's brick industry helped construct many buildings. Lake View's Black Hawk Lake became a major tourist attraction. Odebolt grew because of the two nearby bonanza farms. Early and Wall Lake developed because of the railroad industry. Schaller profited from the popcorn industry. Lytton and Nemaha became agricultural centers. Sac City grew because of commerce, banking, real estate investment, and being a county seat.

Investing in education has been a priority for county residents. In addition to schools in each community, there were one-room schools placed throughout the rural area, so no student had to travel more than two miles to attend classes. The country schools prepared students to pass the eighth grade examination and served as gathering places for rural families. Beautiful churches were focal points for every community. Picturesque country churches often had itinerate ministers who nurtured faith and united families into a close-knit community. Many schools offered adult night school classes that taught adults about new agricultural practices, food preparation, and topics of general interest. The Sac City Institute was a Baptist college that trained teachers and had a well-respected conservatory of music.

In addition to church and school functions, entertainment opportunities included numerous movie theaters, opera houses in several communities, traveling circuses, fishing, hunting, skating, and going to Chautauqua shows. The Chautauqua movement in Sac City was housed in a large pavilion that remains as a significant example of outdoor auditoriums in the state.

Transportation was a major driving force for community growth. Railroad access helped farmers sell commodities, brought products into the county, and allowed residents to travel. Trains brought summer visitors to Black Hawk Lake. When railroad tracks appeared two miles north of Early's original location, the entire town moved to meet the railroad. Highway 20, the longest road in the United States, runs through the northern part of the county, connecting Sac County to the Atlantic and Pacific Oceans.

# One

# Building Community

When the first settlers arrived in Sac County, the allure of rich farmland, ample water, and favorable topography encouraged locating in the area and building communities. Houses, schools, churches, government buildings, and downtown districts gradually emerged from the prairie grass and open spaces. By 1900, most communities had erected churches, schools, and commercial shopping areas. Country schools, churches, and rural stores served as gathering places for close-knit groups of friends and neighbors. Some communities incorporated into towns and cities.

Homes, schools, main streets, and government buildings became defining elements of the various communities in Sac County. Each had at least a few showcase homes that became outward expressions of prosperity. One-room country schools nurtured students and became gathering places for area residents. Relatively small rural churches allowed people to form a faith community without traveling long distances in inclement weather. Schools and churches in incorporated communities tended to be larger and more elaborate. As connections between rural residents and town centers became less challenging to navigate, many of the neighborhood amenities fell by the wayside. By the time of the Great Depression, economic conditions had made maintaining small schools and churches increasingly challenging.

Communities of all sizes took great pride in the identifying structures they had united to build. Whether a small township hall or a large courthouse, there was no doubt that cooperative efforts (and oftentimes a degree of dissent among friends) had played an important role in building Sac County and its communities.

Main Street development was a vital part of building community. An 1896 view of Sac City's Main Street shows the wooden storefronts along dirt streets. There were no streetlights before the turn of the century. Bicycles and horses were the primary means of transport. This photograph is one of the earliest documents of Sac County downtown business districts.

Some businesses had branches in several Sac County towns. W.J. Dixon Lumber began in Sac City but had outlets in Nemaha and Lytton. Seeing the man with a ladder on a utility pole is a strong reminder of how much change has occurred over the past century. Today, the Occupational Safety and Health Administration (OSHA) would certainly suggest a different approach to repairing the line on Lytton's Main Street.

One of the hallmarks of Sac County towns is the unity people develop as they gather for celebrations. It is interesting to note that more people are visible in this 1909 Nemaha gathering than lived in the community at the time. Visiting others was an important element of community growth.

The juxtaposition of wood-frame buildings and imposing masonry structures on Millinery Avenue in Wall Lake is a graphic story of the way Sac County communities developed. Original buildings used native woods for construction materials. As fire or time ravaged the early stores, they were replaced with more permanent brick buildings.

Ornate commercial buildings characterized downtown Early in 1909. The elevated sidewalks were ideal for people dismounting a horse or getting out of a wagon. Several buildings had upper-story living quarters, which frequently helped business owners make small-town stores financially viable. Below, several wooden buildings on the east side of the street seem much more modest but do characterize early commercial structures in many towns.

Country and town certainly meet in this 1912 image on Early's Main Street. The coexistence of automobiles and a cattle-drawn wagon on the same street was not the norm for most towns. The onlookers appear more than slightly skeptical of the thought of harnessing cattle.

Pictured is a portion of the Lake View business district. In the foreground are wood-frame buildings, and in the background is a water tower on a hill. The Hotel Windsor and adjacent Lunch Room welcomed visitors in 1912. Steps on the exterior of a building probably indicate the second story was used as a residential space.

Lake View has always been more than a lake. The wide Main Street business district serviced residents throughout the year and tourists during the summer months. This 1911 view shows the modern streetlights that helped assure safety for pedestrians.

Lake View's Main Street was lined with rather ornate brick buildings. Drivers had not yet developed a consistent method of parking. Some preferred parallel parking, and others opted for angled parking. Five-globe streetlights helped pedestrians find the elevated crosswalks to cross the dirt streets.

Business districts are constructed one building at a time. An early-1890s view of Auburn's Main Street shows wooden sidewalks and a dirt street with a pond big enough to have a man rowing a small boat in front of a group of spectators. Citizens complaining about street conditions is not a new phenomenon.

Railroad tracks, sidewalks, a hotel, and even a bandstand welcomed visitors to Auburn in 1909. The brick hotel may have been constructed using bricks from the Auburn brick and tile plant. The striking pattern along the top of the building at left typifies the attention to detail that characterized early-20th-century architecture in Sac County.

Main Street Lytton (around 1910) was filled with wood-frame commercial buildings and dirt streets. Concrete sidewalks provided easy passage for pedestrians as they visited the various stores. The grain elevator at the end of the street, near the railroad, serves as a wonderful reminder of the interdependence of the town and the farm community that still exists in Lytton.

Clothing stores, a dentist, and jewelers greeted customers who traveled in horse-drawn transport to Schaller's Second Street business district. Hitching posts served as safe parking spaces for the horses while people enjoyed the opportunity to socialize and purchase goods that could not be grown on the farm.

Odebolt's Princess Theater shows the 1914 silent film *Rescued by Wireless*, starring William Clifford and Marie Walcamp. Watching a film set in Hawaii, complete with a thrilling rescue, a love triangle, and fascinating island scenery, helped quench Sac County residents' thirst for glamour and excitement. Model Market, next to the theater, offered quality meats to satisfy hungry appetites developed from hours of physical labor.

Main Street business districts provided shoppers the opportunity to explore many stores in close proximity. When a fire broke out in one building, firefighters had to work to contain the blaze. This scene, looking east on Sac City's Main Street, shows the community effort to save adjacent properties from fire damage. Even though fire was a tragedy, it was an impetus for business owners to upgrade wooden buildings to masonry structures that were less prone to fire damage.

This view of Sac City Main Street, around 1915, is a reminder that automobiles and horses existed comfortably together as means of transportation. Dirt streets were commonplace for most cities. High curbs helped keep dust away from pedestrians, and wooden sidewalks kept long dresses from dragging in the mud. During rainy seasons, the street's sharp incline became difficult for automobile traffic.

The number of people and businesses on the corner of Sixth and Main Streets in Sac City is almost overwhelming. Some of the stores include a candy kitchen, which sold candy, ice cream, refreshments, and news periodicals; Wilson's Drugs; a wallpaper store; and the Dew Drop Inn restaurant. Also visible are Masonic lodge symbols, brick streets, ornate lights, and randomly parked cars, providing a striking background for the bustling groups of people and knicker-clad children.

Without people, there would be no communities. In 1934, the Wycoff family added significantly to Sac City's population when their famous quadruplets were born, bringing the family size to nine children. Lester, LaVerne, LaVonne, and Lorraine joined, from left to right, Lawrence Sr., Lawrence Jr. (7), Charles (6), Bobbie (4), Lois (3), Norma (18 months), and Ida. Large families contributed to the need for many new schools. Not all families were as prolific as the Wycoffs, and the 19 students attending a one-room country school near Lake View in the image at right would have lived on farms within four square miles.

Sac City Institute was the only college in Sac County. Founded in 1895, the investors selected the county seat town because it was "free from temptations to idleness and vice. There are no saloons, billiard halls, or gambling places." Academy Hall, on the right, housed six classrooms, a chapel, the principal's office, a society hall, the library, and a cloak room. The building on the left was a women's dormitory, and Platt Hall (back center) served as a men's dormitory. The institute closed in 1912.

This close view of the Sac City Institute Academy Hall highlights some of the architectural features of the building. The combination of square windows, arched doorways, and a square tower with a rather odd rounded turret attached is as eclectic as the academic offerings at the college. Admitting children as young as 10 years of age, it offered teacher certification programs and musical training in a conservatory setting.

Grant City was one of the earliest settlements in Sac County. The 1856 mill was the first in the county. The town finally incorporated in 1904 to provide better funding for its school. Grant City was purported to have the best roller-skating rink in Northwest Iowa. Without railroad access, the town quickly declined and even lost postal service by 1912. This is a 1907 view of its fine brick school.

Nemaha's high school, pictured around 1915, served as an education center for not only students in town, but also many from the rural area who had graduated from eighth grade in one-room country schools. At one time, every community had a high school, which is in stark contrast to the present day when there is only one high school in the county.

Wall Lake has a strong tradition of supporting its schools. The four-room school was enlarged in 1903 after voters approved a bond issue and a 10 mill tax increase (a mill is $1 tax per $1,000 taxable valuation). To put that in perspective, the average annual salary was $450 and the average home price was $5,000, making it a tax increase of $50 a year to support the school.

The fine 1906 brick-and-stone school in Schaller is a testament to county residents' willingness to invest in public education. For students accustomed to one-room rural schools, attending high school in such an impressive building was certainly an adjustment. The tube-like fire escape was typical for many schools in Sac County.

The wooden high school in Early (above) was constructed in 1883. The two rooms on the main floor sufficed until enrollment grew to 45 students, at which time the rooms on the second story were finished. In 1915, the school consolidated with nearby districts, creating a need for much more space. The community passed a $75,000 bond issue and built the brick school seen below, which served the community until it was destroyed by an explosion and fire in 1982.

23

The first large school in Sac City was constructed on the south side of Main Street between Sixth and Seventh Streets. County residents' value for education is reflected in the architectural detail of this 1880s building. Arched windows, ornate corbels, a carefully constructed cupola, and round windows in the attic make this school one of the most striking examples of Richardsonian Romanesque architecture erected in Sac County. The community soon outgrew the school and constructed a white wood-frame building for additional classrooms before erecting a new larger school several blocks west in 1903.

The 1900 wood-frame high school in Lytton was basically a two-story version of typical country schools. Residents decided to build a school and assumed financial responsibility for the $2,500 cost even before the town had any elected officials. There were two rooms on the main floor with a central stairway leading to the one-room second story.

The two-story wooden school in Lake View, constructed around 1900, housed both elementary and high school students. In addition to learning traditional subjects, students became quite adept at firefighting, as sparks from the chimney often set the building on fire. It is unusual to see chimneys shorter than the tallest part of the building.

Outside recess was a staple for all elementary students. Games and camaraderie developed lifelong friendships. Older students mentored younger learners in and out of the classroom, which helped country schools, like this one in Clinton Township, provide quality education to students in eight grade levels. Teachers were responsible for all subjects as well as supervising recess and games, cleaning the school, and starting the fire to warm the building in winter months.

In 1908, Sac City students sit attentively at desks attached to the floor. Each desk had an inkwell. More than one student was disciplined for dipping someone's hair in the black ink. Students learned proper penmanship in addition to the traditional "three Rs"—reading, writing, and arithmetic. Class sizes of more than 30 students were not uncommon.

What could make more sense than climbing onto the roof of a three-story school building and gathering around the cupola for a class picture? Sac City students in 1910 certainly were not acrophobic, as the photograph shows an entire group with broad smiles, something relatively rare for photographs of that era.

The school between Tenth and Eleventh Streets on Sac City's Main Street had one of the first indoor swimming pools in any school in Iowa. The hand-dug and tiled pool was a source of great pride for the community. One of the hallmark activities was a synchronized swimming performance known as the Dolphin Show. The pool, still in use today as part of the Sac Community Center, continues to teach young children to swim and to offer adults the opportunity to exercise in the winter months.

Following an 1888 fire that destroyed the previous courthouse, the Sac County Courthouse was constructed in 1889. There were efforts from some towns to relocate the county seat; local businessmen donated $15,000 to match the insurance settlement from the old building and erected this structure using plans drawn by J.M. Russel of Storm Lake. The plans had been used to build the Buena Vista County Courthouse. The 1899 view shows the original cupola that was later removed, as evidenced by the 1920s photograph. Although the Storm Lake building has been razed, the Sac County Courthouse is still in use and listed in the National Register of Historic Places.

Court House, Sac City, Iowa

In 1892, the voters in Sac County approved a one mill tax increase to place a monument to the county residents who had served in the Civil War. The statue was erected in the square south of the courthouse in Sac City. Several thousand people attended the dedication ceremony that began with a parade led by Civil War veteran Phil Schaller. The statue still stands as the focal point of the Sac City Monument Square Historic District, listed in the National Register of Historic Places.

Following World War I (known as the Great War), Sac County residents wanted to honor those who had given their lives in war. The Classic Revival American Legion Hall (later known as Community Building or Towne House) honored all county residents killed in service and served as a meeting hall for the American Legion. The stately building, erected in 1922, overlooks the Sac City Monument Square. The Civil War cannon that appears to protect the building was sent away during World War II as a part of the war effort to acquire metal to make war supplies.

The Civil War Monument in Sac City was surrounded by four Civil War cannon. Shortly after the cannon arrived, prominent local veteran Phil Schaller wanted to surprise residents on the Fourth of July. Unfortunately, Schaller had not been trained in artillery and placed too much powder in the cannon. When it fired, the repercussions were strong enough to break most of the windows in the courthouse and in buildings on the north side of Main Street.

Andrew Carnegie's generosity placed libraries in many towns. Sac City's library (above) was the result of his largesse. Iowa architects Proudfoot & Bird designed the brick library that opened in 1912. The Field-Carnegie Library (below) was erected in 1904, making Odebolt the first town with fewer than 5,000 residents to receive a Carnegie Library. In addition to offering educational opportunities, libraries often served as gathering places for the community.

Odebolt Public Library, Odebolt, Iowa.

Volunteer fire departments not only worked to save properties from fire damage, but also spent countless hours training men to improve their firefighting skills. Part of that training involved participating in competitions with other departments. In this 1909 real-photo postcard, Kelly's Colts from the Odebolt Fire Department show their pride after winning awards.

Fire protection is a critical need for any community. Every town in Sac County organized volunteer fire departments, which worked diligently to protect buildings that were typically constructed of wood, built close together, and heated with burning wood and coal. Sac City had two fire departments because it was difficult to transport equipment on the steep Main Street hill. These Sac City volunteers pose with an early hose trailer about 1905.

Water supply is a vital need for every community. Underground pipes, treatment plants, and wells are neither glamorous nor noticed. A town's water tower, however, becomes much more than a part of the utility; its shape serves as a recognizable symbol to identify the city, as evidenced by the desire to feature them on postcards. Sac City's cylindrical tower (right), photographed around 1900, supplied water for many years. Wall Lake opted for a more traditional shape when replacing the original wooden tower in 1912 (below).

Mail service provides connections with people throughout the world. For people vacationing at Cottage Grove in Lake View, letters from friends and relatives were exciting to receive. In 1911, the postman delivered mail in a horse-drawn buggy.

Lake cottages were often simpler and smaller than other residences. Most were used only in the summer months. The limited quantity of lakeshore caused the cottages to be built quite close together. In many cases, the owners of the cottages leased the land on which their summer homes sat.

Homes in Sac County were as varied as the residents themselves. The amazing symmetry of the three gables on the front of the J.W. Hartsell house in Early is unusual. Incorporating stained glass into windows was common practice in the early 1900s.

Charles Goodnow's residence in Wall Lake incorporated both symmetry and architectural detail into a beautifully maintained home. The contrasting paint colors were typical of many early-20th-century buildings. The decorative filigree wood pieces and different types of siding make what could have been a rather plain home become a work of art.

Tree-lined residential streets characterize most Sac County towns. Open porches allowed residents the opportunity to enjoy nature and interact with neighbors. The area's ample rainfall and growing seasons are ideal for many types of deciduous trees, which grace the spacious front yards. Many homes from the early part of the 20th century have open porches like these gracious examples in Schaller (above) and Auburn (below). Brick sidewalks were not uncommon in some areas.

Residence of A.L. Manly.

A.L. Manly's farm residence, south of Early, was a fine example of a modern home in a rural setting. The large open porch was a comfortable place for family gatherings. As farming became more profitable, many owners built new homes. This 1919 photograph was taken soon after Manly (standing next to pillar) built the house.

No. 7          Residence of G. S. Needham,          Early, Iowa.

The stately Needham house in Early was one of the area's finest dwellings. After the Needhams sold the home, the Rutledge family lived there for many years. The Rutledges founded Farmers Mutual Hail Insurance Co., said to be the largest such company in the world. Hail insurance helped provide financial stability for farmers in the event of crop failure.

George and Lola Perkins built this stately home on Sac City's Main Street in 1912. It is one of the last houses designed by mail order architect George Barber, who published catalogs of house plans. Lola Perkins communicated with Barber to modify the design to fit on the relatively small corner lot. The Classic Revival structure remains in use as a private residence and is listed in the National Register of Historic Places.

Eli and Amie Baily were prominent Sac City bankers. Eli Baily was very active in the development of the Sac City Library and the Chautauqua movements. In 1893, they built Seven Oaks atop Audubon Street hill. Notable Iowa architects Proudfoot & Bird designed the sunporches that adorned the home planned by J.M. Russel of Storm Lake. Baily equipped the property with a generator, making it the first home in the area with electricity. The home is listed in the National Register of Historic Places.

D. Carr Early, one of Sac City's first settlers, made his fortune selling real estate and working in the banking industry. His iconic 1874 Second Empire home occupied an entire block on the north side of Sac City's Main Street hill and was among the grandest residences in the county. The stately mansion later became a hospital, apartment building, the well-known Carlson House restaurant, and, once again, a private home.

Many storefronts, including the Red Cross Pharmacy on Main Street in Sac City, had awnings to protect not only those wanting to enjoy the view of passersby, but also the items in the store windows from the harsh sunlight. Basement windows allowed enough light for barbershops, lounges, and other commercial interests on the lower level of many buildings. In addition to medicines, this store also specialized in stationery and perfumes.

A lunchroom near a train depot became an important hangout for traveling salesmen and railroad workers. The weather must have been hot this day; most of the men have shed their coats and donned straw hats. The five gentlemen took time for a quick photograph around 1920 near the Chicago, Milwaukee & St. Paul Depot on North Fifth Street in Sac City.

Sac City jeweler H.W. Alexander was an expert silversmith. At the turn of the 20th century, he created hundreds of sterling spoons with intricately carved images of local landmarks. These spoons were popular gifts for confirmations and graduations. Visitors to the community were frequently directed to the store on Williams Street with the large pocket watch to purchase souvenirs.

Having a town hall is a vital part of building a community. Odebolt's town hall combined office space with a garage area. The bell above the building rang out to call volunteer firefighters. Dr. Gramin's office was right next door in case the city council meetings became too exciting.

Wooden commercial buildings were typically the first constructed in most communities. Many had retail space on the main floor and living quarters on the upper story. E.E. Smith and Company in Nemaha was a proud outlet for Huiskamp Shoes, which were made in Keokuk, Iowa. The photograph was taken after 1907 when telephone service came to the community.

A variety store was an important part of every thriving business community. Lake View's variety store advertises candy and displays sets of dishes and decorative glassware in its windows. The beautiful lead glass transom windows above the display windows were a common feature for many early-1900 storefronts in Sac County.

# Two

# BUILDING AGRICULTURE AND INDUSTRY

The desire for prosperity drew many people to Sac County. The first settlers had to rely on ingenuity and business savvy to survive. Without an adequate food supply, the harsh Iowa prairie winters would have been impossible to survive. Farmers began to search for the best crops and livestock to feed themselves and their neighbors. This quest helped develop farming practices in Sac County that would change the future of agriculture. Both the Adams Ranch and the Cook Ranch explored new management techniques to maximize productivity and profits.

Sawmills transformed native timber into usable lumber; gristmills ground flour and corn; merchants sold goods to residents; land agents profited from sales; canning companies and food processing plants helped preserve and share the bountiful crops; bankers, lawyers, doctors, and a host of professionals opened shops; and the county began to prosper. When farmers realized that popcorn was ideally suited for the climate, several popcorn companies not only processed the crop, but also helped market it on a broad scale.

The partnership between agriculture and business transformed Sac County from a fledgling area into a land of prosperity. Over the decades, the county developed a good balance of agriculture and industry that remains to this day.

Natural clay deposits along the North Raccoon River near Auburn provided an ideal opportunity to make bricks and tiles to help Sac County and the surrounding area grow. These 1909 images show workers loading the kilns and the small-gauge rail track that helped transport materials to the kilns and carry finished bricks out of the area. Many buildings that graced main streets throughout the county featured locally produced brick from kilns east of Auburn.

In addition to Auburn, other county towns produced clay products. Drainage tile was especially important to the agricultural industry, as it allowed better drainage to transform wetlands into arable farmland. As the demand for agricultural products increased, the demand for tile increased. This stockpile of tile, pictured around 1910, is adjacent to the Sac City tile plant.

The Sac City Canning Company purchased sweetcorn and peas from area farmers. The produce was processed and canned before being sold to grocery outlets. The factory employed many seasonal workers and helped diversify the agricultural economy. The company was located on the northwest side of Sac City.

Wayt Monument Company in Sac City supplied granite tombstones throughout Northwest Iowa. After coming to Sac City in 1889, the company opened this location on the corner of South Fifth and Audubon Streets in 1893. The company constructed the Wayt Monument building on the corner of Thirteenth and Main Streets in 1914. The new location, adjacent to the Chicago & Northwestern Railroad, allowed them to easily receive granite shipments and deliver completed monuments.

Before refrigeration was commonplace, protecting food from spoilage was a challenge. Many homes had iceboxes that required frequent deliveries of ice. C.M. Mohler harvested ice from the lake and preserved it in sawdust so families could eat safely and enjoy cold foods throughout the year.

Sac County has large natural deposits of gravel that resulted from glacial movement. Removing the gravel from pits and selling it has proven to be a profitable endeavor. Steam shovels and short private rail lines were essential tools for the industry that continues to this day. One interesting byproduct of the process is water-filled pits, which have become significant recreational areas.

Elaborate equipment helped haul gravel out of the gravel pits. The Quirk family was active in the sand and gravel business around Lake View. Two well-dressed men, whose shoes suggest they did not work in the dusty gravel, pose beside the platform at the top of the gravel pit around 1915.

Providing utilities to a community is vital for growth. The Sac County Electrical Plant in Sac City certainly made lives easier. Switching from gas or kerosene lighting to electrical changed every community. The first home in Sac City to have electric lighting was Seven Oaks, built in 1893; the home's private generator helped create a demand for a public electric utility. The electrical plant was located on the north side of Main Street, near the Chicago & Northwestern Depot, which allowed for ready access to coal to produce electricity.

As fewer town residents kept their own cows, local dairies began making daily deliveries. Sac City Dairy bought milk and cream from area farmers, bottled it, and transported it to local homes. In an era when refrigeration was provided by iceboxes, having a ready supply of fresh milk was a necessity for many homes.

Agriculture drove town economies throughout Sac County. Most towns had at least one creamery that purchased milk or cream from farmers. The Sac City Creamery, located just east of the Sac City Monument Square, helped supply milk and cream to local residents with door-to-door deliveries. The blacksmith shop to the right made horseshoes that protected many of the horses used in farming throughout the area.

Developing markets for crops is an important part of farming. Railroads provided a way to expand markets. The time spent waiting to unload wagons became a social time for the exchange of ideas. This scene, looking south on North Fifth Street in Sac City, shows not only the juxtaposition of rail and horse-drawn transport, but also the interaction of rural and city that helped shape Sac County.

One industry in Sac City was the Kurtz Product company, which made this steel-tired Motorall. The tractor had a maximum speed of five miles per hour and generated 40 horsepower. Samuel Kurtz's 1902 patent for a motorized plow was jointly owned by Kurtz and Albert Cook, manager and owner of Odebolt's 7,680-acre Brookmont Farm, which was commonly called the Cook Ranch.

The Iowa Railroad Land Company aggressively marketed farmland to wealthy investors. Two large bonanza farms near Odebolt were the result of this marketing. Chicagoan Charles Willard Cook purchased 12 sections of land (7,680 acres) in 1873, establishing the Cook Ranch. In 1872, Hiram Cyrus Wheeler purchased 7,000 acres using insurance money from losses in the Great Chicago Fire. Wheeler's land eventually became the Adams Ranch, also known as Fairview Farm. Large-scale operations helped pioneer modern farming practices. Adams Ranch operated using mules and had dormitories for workers. Overseers lived in small homes. The farm was essentially a small town with its own water tower and fire protection.

The Adams family lived in a large home on the ranch. They enjoyed their own swimming pool. The ranch had its own elevator to store grain and a shop to repair all the equipment. The ears of corn lying on the desk in Adams's rather ornate office are a testament to the careful study of farming practices that made the ranch successful. Many people visited the ranch to learn about studies in plant genetics and animal husbandry. W.P. Adams's efforts helped pave the way for modern farming practices.

Learning about modern agricultural practices was commonplace in Odebolt. W.P. Adams's 7,000-acre ranch attracted many visitors who provided an economic boon for the town. In 1910, this caravan from the land grant university in Ames (now Iowa State University) traveled to Odebolt and enjoyed many of the community's businesses.

Boosters from the land grant university in Ames (now Iowa State University) often visited the Adams Ranch. The information they learned there helped shape agricultural practices throughout the state. The automobiles are parked by the large barn on the ranch, where students could have a firsthand look at modern animal science practices.

The stately Neoclassical bank building in Odebolt was the result of W.P. Adams's efforts. He maintained a private office in the bank that was a vital part of his large-scale farming operation. In 1912, the town enjoyed a sense of opulence that was atypical for towns in rural Iowa.

Sawmills, like this one in Odebolt, were vital businesses to transform the presettlement trees into lumber used to build communities. Workers used axes and metal wedges to split logs as well as tractor-powered saws to create a product that changed the landscape of every part of Sac County. This 1918 mill on the Adams Ranch used Mennonite Conscientious Objectors to help clear dead cottonwood trees and transport the wood to a box company.

The Cook Ranch, also known as Brookmont Farm, began when Charles Cook purchased 12 sections (7,680 acres) of Sac County land in 1873. The farm was divided into 24 half-section farms, each with a complete set of farm buildings and its own tenant. In 1883, Cook imported Hereford cattle from England and began the line of Brookmont Herefords. He built a large home, which burned in the 1890s. A.E. Cook, son of the original owner, built this smaller home to replace it.

Sac County was a wonderful place to raise quality livestock. Bountiful corn and pastureland helped produce fine cattle, hogs, and sheep. A farmer who had prizewinning animals was able to sell at a premium. Livestock shows were not only popular entertainment, but also a way to increase the value of a herd. This Sac County farmer's pride is evident as he prepares his prize steer for the show ring.

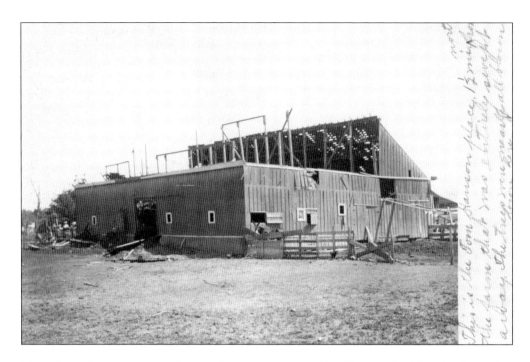

Tornados in Sac County can do great damage to crops and buildings. Rebuilding this barn after tornado damage in 1907 was not only costly, but may have seemed futile. The desire for new and better farming practices characterized Sac County agriculture. Building maintenance can be a costly endeavor. The barn, shown in this 1911 photograph below, was made from anchor black and eliminated the need for painting and was certainly more structurally sound than most wood-sided barns.

Tornados are not the only risk to structures. Fire could destroy a building very quickly in 1912. The fire at the Einspahr Garage in Odebolt, with its billowing black smoke, raged on as helpless onlookers lamented the loss of a local business.

Fires are an inherent danger with grain storage. If grain is too wet, the heat from fermentation will start a fire. Grain dust can explode and ignite a building. The best efforts of Odebolt and area firefighters could not save the Trans-Mississippi Popcorn Elevator from this 1913 fire. The fire caused more than $50,000 in damage.

NATIONAL OATS PLANT. WALL LAKE. IOWA

Popcorn processing came to Wall Lake in 1927 when August Fischer and Carl Erne opened the Popcorn Growers and Distributors business. The firm's initial location burned to the ground that same year. The partners persevered and built this facility, which was sold to National Oats Company in 1955.

Popcorn has been a Sac County staple for many years. The Odebolt area grew most of the popcorn used to make Cracker Jack. Storing popcorn in well-ventilated cribs helped assure the kernels maintained proper moisture content so the corn would pop into large, fluffy, delicious treats to share with friends. Cracker Jack began operating in Odebolt in 1918.

Ringgenberg Implement in Lytton opened in 1901, selling all types of farm machinery, sleds, and buggies. The Harter, Wilson, and Bromwell Company from Sac City purchased the business in 1910. Farm implement stores helped build the partnership between towns and the rural residents. Without this partnership, no Sac County city would have survived.

There is nothing like an auction sale to bring people together. In this 1911 Nemaha scene, friends and neighbors gather to witness the sale of sewing machines, kitchen cabinets, tables, and even empty barrels. Whether the owner died or was moving, there was certainly an element of sadness as people said goodbye to friends and hello to new belongings.

The Civilian Conservation Corps (CCC) was one of Franklin D. Roosevelt's most successful programs. Men were paid for manual labor related to the conservation and development of natural resources on public lands. The workers lived in camps like this one in Lake View. The workers made many improvements in the area, including to the stone piers on Black Hawk Lake. The piers are listed in the National Register of Historic Places.

Beautiful commercial buildings were the hallmark of any progressive town. J.M. Fox's building, located on the southwest corner of Fifth and Main Streets in Sac City, provided retail space, a barbershop on the lower level, and residential quarters on the upper story. The ornate brickwork is a wonderful testament to the pride of ownership many proprietors showed in their communities.

The combination of furniture maker and undertaker was commonplace in most communities. Building coffins and furniture was one way to diversify income. W.R. Temple, on the north side of Main Street in Sac City, had a lucrative business. The shipment of mattresses helped meet the needs of a growing community whose ability to purchase mattresses rather than using homemade straw-filled ones was a testament to the increasing affluence in Sac County in the early 1900s.

When railroads came into town, business districts often expanded to meet the railroad. This small row of stores on Early Street in Sac City was only a block from the Chicago & Northwestern Depot. Dry goods, groceries, a meat market, and a small restaurant offered train travelers the opportunity to purchase items on a short layover and provided a place for those waiting for a train to shop. This neighborhood commercial district also helped people avoid traveling up and down Main Street's steep hill during winter months.

The unincorporated town of Ulmer began as an Illinois Railroad stop. Several businesses opened after the town was platted in 1900. The 1910 advertising card for the Farmers' Savings Bank asserts, "Your name would look well in our books. Open your account today." The ornate woodwork certainly gives a feeling of prosperity.

Restaurants are an important service industry. The dining room of the Park Hotel in Sac City was a popular gathering place for social clubs, children's birthday parties, and hotel patrons. T-bone steak was the most popular menu item, and dinner knives were the most popular item removed from the restaurant as souvenirs. One year, the owners had to replace more than 600 knives. The art glass panels in the swinging doors leading to the kitchen helped add to the room's elegance and reputation for fine dining in the 1920s.

Hospitality work provided many jobs. The Park Hotel's lobby featured an ornate tile floor and a white counter made of marble from the same quarry as that used for the Lincoln Memorial. The phone booth provided privacy for guests to contact home. The porter was always ready to help carry luggage to the second or third floor. Many of the hotel's workers lived on the fourth floor and received lodging as a part of their pay.

Stonebrook's dry goods store in Sac City offered a variety of fabrics and sewing supplies for every seamstress. Hand-painted plates and souvenir china with pictures of local buildings were popular in the early 1900s. The store even sold real-photo postcards like this one. Judging by the large cigar and pipe display, one wonders how many times the fabric needed to be washed to rid of the tobacco aroma that must have filled the store.

A butcher's scale was one of his most important tools. The interior of Zahnhiser's Meat Market on the corner of State and Main Streets in Sac City displays hanging hams, refrigerated meats, and a variety of wrapping papers and string to protect shoppers' purchases. In an era when home refrigeration was limited, a ready supply of fresh meat was vital for every community.

H.R. Stanzel purchased the Selby and Pottinger drug and jewelry store in 1917. The Odebolt store carried beautiful glassware and jewelry. This real-photo postcard was given to customers as a token of appreciation with the hope that it would be mailed to friends who would opt to come to Odebolt and shop in Stanzel's impeccably organized store.

Shopping has changed significantly since 1914. Finding four clerks in a relatively small retail space was not uncommon in an era when customers were not allowed to pick up their own items. Glass cases and items stacked nearly to the ceiling typified many stores like this one on Sac City's Main Street.

Lunch counters were popular gathering places in every community. As a location to take a break from shopping, meeting a friend, or waiting for one of the movies advertised on the wall, downtown restaurants provided an essential service for residents and visitors. Ice cream cones and orange soda were only a nickel in 1940 in Sac City.

Recycling is not a new concept. This Model A traveled from house to house in Sac City collecting newspaper and tin cans to be sold. A.L. Manly managed to fill the car nearly every day. Although there was a small profit for his efforts, the desire to conserve resources was the underlying reason for his efforts. Entrepreneurship and creativity helped build a variety of business and industry in Sac County.

# *Three*

# BUILDING FOR PLEASURE

Sac County has many opportunities for enjoyment. The beauty of Black Hawk Lake and the North Raccoon River creates natural playgrounds. As the county developed, people capitalized on these areas to attract visitors and provide entertainment for area residents. Boats, waterslides, and lakeshore homes were a natural outgrowth of a prosperous economy. The area became known as a destination for hunting and fishing.

Church events, school performances, and athletics have always been a great source of pleasure. Libraries not only expanded minds, but also offered the escape of great books to fill idle times. Fraternal organizations erected buildings for their meetings. Investors built opera houses to host community gatherings and touring performers.

The Chautauqua movement offered entertainment each summer. Sac City's unique Chautauqua pavilion remains a monument to the movement Teddy Roosevelt termed "the most American thing in America."

The Sac County Fair brought visitors from miles around to celebrate agricultural greatness and be entertained by daredevils, races, rides, and performers.

Throughout its history, Sac County has developed a remarkable tradition of using leisure activities to improve creativity, expand minds, and attract visitors. If the adage "all work and no play make Jack a dull boy" is true, the only dull people in the county were those who chose to ignore the many options to fill leisure hours.

CATHOLIC
CHURCH

WALL LAKE, IA.

Churches played a vital role in the development of Sac County. St. Joseph's Catholic Church in Wall Lake built this 100-seat church in 1905 after the previous one was destroyed by fire in 1904. The 34-by-85-foot building had a gallery in the sanctuary and meeting rooms in the basement. Construction cost was $4,800, not including the price of furnishings. Frank Lee of Denison was the contractor for the building.

St. Mary's Catholic Church and rectory in Auburn typifies small-town commitment to building beautiful houses of worship. Catholics built a church near Auburn before the town existed. Building the present church in 1921 was a great accomplishment, solemnized in a public dedicatory mass by Bishop Heelan, 26 priests, and more people than would fit in the richly adorned sanctuary. The intricate paintings and statuary inside the church typify many area Catholic churches of the early 1900s.

Churches helped define every community. The admonition to "remember the Sabbath and keep it holy" mandated that no store would be open on Sunday. Schaller's first Methodist church (above), built in 1883, cost $4,000. It was the congregation's home until a brick building was dedicated in 1911. The Presbyterian church (left) was built in 1890 at a cost of $3,036.49. Members had contributed all but $500 of the cost prior to the dedication.

A picturesque wooden church with a central steeple is quintessential Americana. The Methodist church in Grant City sits nestled in a grove of trees, inviting worshippers to experience a unique combination of community and solitude. By 1909, Grant City's fortune was declining.

In July 1889, a wood-frame church was built two miles northwest of Nemaha. The building was moved into Nemaha and dedicated July 16, 1900. This structure served the Nemaha Methodists until 1919, when the congregation decided to build a brick church rather than spend the money to repair the wooden one. The Methodist church has shaped the lives of generations of Nemaha residents.

Laying a cornerstone is always a special event. A building's cornerstone typically housed memorabilia intended to be examined if the structure were razed. The congregation of the Methodist church in Lake View did not allow rainy conditions to dampen the excitement of the event. Months of careful work finally resulted in the completed house of worship.

A rural church and a country school are potent reminders of the importance of farming neighborhoods. During the week, students gathered to learn and improve their minds; on Sundays, all gathered to improve their spirits. Having churches and schools nearby was important, especially during the cold winter months when transportation was challenging.

The Presbyterian church was the only church in Ulmer. It served as a gathering place and community center as well as a house of worship. This 1911 photograph shows one of the few streets in this town that served an important role for the surrounding agricultural community.

During World War I, patriotism was very high. Even churches displayed American flags to demonstrate allegiance to country. The juxtaposition of God and country in this Lytton church is a testament to Sac County's historic values: uniting people into one community, worshiping together, and supporting the military.

Sacred Heart Catholic Church in Early has served the community since 1884. Parishioners built the brick house of worship in 1899 at a cost of $15,000. As shown in this 1909 photograph, the interior's curved vaulted ceiling and decorative altars were quite spectacular. The church still serves the Catholic community today.

Country churches united neighbors into one close-knit body. Pleasant Hill Methodist Church in rural Early served not only as a house of worship, but also a community gathering place. Several congregants produced a play in the church to entertain the neighborhood. Seeing people in blackface is a grim reminder that racial sensitivity was not a consideration in 1915.

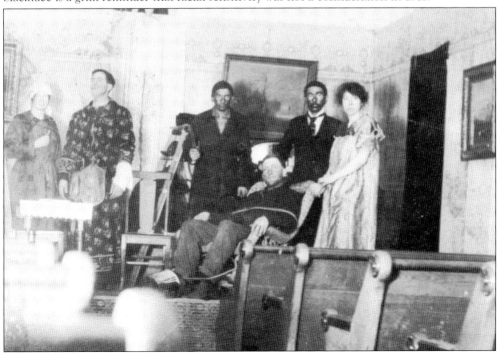

The Methodist Episcopal Church (now United Methodist) formed its first congregation in Sac County when the Sac City church formed in 1855. Tradition states that Isabella Cory crossed the North Raccoon River, ascended the hill, and knelt to pray on the site of the present church. The 1903 edifice, as shown here, was constructed according to the Akron plan. The octagonal sanctuary opened to classroom space, optimizing the building for worship and extensive Sunday school classes. The congregation was one of 10 Methodist churches in the county.

Constructing churches was an important part of building communities. Members of the First Christian Church in Sac City gathered to celebrate Rally Day, which kicked off the fall season of Sunday school. The combination of rambunctious children, beautifully clad women, and stoic men certainly created an interesting dynamic on this special day around 1910.

Some buildings undergo significant transformations. When the Sac City Baptists decided to construct a new church in 1911, they sold their old building to the Free Methodist congregation. The Free Methodists moved the building from Main Street to Early Street, placed it on a new foundation, and moved the door, investing in a church structure that would serve the congregation for its entire life.

General Sherman Hall in Sac City is one of the few remaining Grand Army of the Republic (GAR) buildings in Iowa. The organization of Civil War veterans built the Classic Revival structure in 1892 and received permission to name it after the famous Civil War general, who had died the year before. Like all GAR organizations, Post No. 284 ceased as the last local Civil War veterans died. The building is listed in the National Register of Historic Places and currently serves as a senior citizen's center.

Sac County residents hold veterans in high esteem. Several GAR posts united veterans of the Civil War. Large gatherings of those who helped preserve the Union, such as this 1907 celebration in the Sac City Monument Square surrounding the taxpayer-approved soldier monument, were common events. Several reunions brought thousands of veterans and their families to the area.

Fraternal organizations offered social interaction and contributed to the betterment of communities. The Independent Order of Odd Fellows (IOOF) had lodges in every county town but Nemaha. Lodges often had meeting rooms on the upper floors and commercial space on the main floor. Sac City's IOOF building (above) had a movie theater on the main floor for many years. The lodge hall in Lytton (below) also served as the town's opera house.

The opera house in Sac City (front left) was literally the cornerstone of the business district. Small-town opera houses typically had retail space on the lower levels and a large room with a stage on the upper level. High school students often rented the space for parties, but adults always had to sample the punch before the celebration could begin. The building, located at the northeast corner of Sixth and Main Streets, was destroyed by fire in 1939. The Masons built their lodge adjacent to the opera house.

Wall Lake's opera house, like those in other towns, was an important gathering place. School programs, community performances, parties, and informational meetings were commonplace events. Local investors purchased stock to fund the 1912 construction; the building was opened with a local production of the play *The White Lie*. Some who were skeptical of investing in an opera house found the play's title more than slightly ironic.

Weekly summer band concerts helped draw rural residents into communities and bring those who lived in town into the commercial district. The concrete block bandstand on the east side of the Sac City Monument Square provided a venue for performances. Hitching posts to the right of the photograph allowed visitors to safely "park" horses while enjoying fun music. Even in 1915, Sac County residents understood that the arts played a significant role in economic development.

The bandstand in Lake View was on the lawn of the Lake View Hotel. Residents and vacationers gather under the trees to hear the local band members share their love of music. The young men seated at the picnic table appear much more interested in watching someone passing by than listening to the music.

People's love of music brings a crowd to Early's Main Street on what appears to be a 1910 Fourth of July celebration with a flag-bedecked automobile. One man is dressed in a shirt and tie with his bib overalls that may have been purchased at the store in the background advertising dry goods, hats, caps, and overalls on its awning.

Community bands not only provided entertainment for local events, but offered an outlet for those who loved to share their musical talent. Odebolt's Gosch-Wilken band (comprised of members of the two families) used the following typical instrumentation for the day: bass drum, snare drum, as many brass players as possible, and one clarinet. It would be interesting to have audio to go with this early-1900s photograph.

Sac City Band.

This Sac City's municipal band posed in front of the Civil War statue in the Sac City Monument Square in the 1920s. During the summer, weekly concerts in the local band shell attracted large crowds. In addition to playing weekly concerts, the band marched in many area parades and was an active part of American Legion events.

Community bands were a good way for communities in Sac County to interact. The opportunity for the Sac City band to tour to Nemaha, even if it was only eight miles away, was a great experience, as can be witnessed by the players who appear to be smiling in this 1909 photograph.

There is nothing like a clown band to attract attention. Front and back views of the band advertising the 1910 Sac County Fair show the fun costumes and handwritten signs inviting people to watch auto races, enjoy pure water, laugh with Silly Bill, meet Little Willie, and (perhaps most importantly) meet girls at the fair. One man dressed as a woman wears a sign promising a date with those who come to the fair.

One can only imagine the potential problems when the marching band follows the horses in a parade. The 1916 Fourth of July parade on Main Street in Sac City provides a wonderful view of the front of the opera house. The small balcony was an ideal location for the young woman to enjoy the passing parade while protecting her fair skin from the sun with a parasol. The high curb helped keep the dust away from pedestrians on the sidewalk.

A car transformed into a float and a farm wagon pulled by horses form part of a Fourth of July parade in Sac City. The brick-paved Main Street was a huge improvement when compared with the previous dirt street that once passed in front of D. Carr Early's magnificent home.

Seeing a circus, complete with live elephants, is every child's dream. A parade of elephants and other exotic animals, accompanied by a steam calliope and circus band, brought great excitement to Sac City and the surrounding towns. A parade on Main Street hill helped build excitement and sell tickets. The profitable 1908 Sac City engagement of the Gollmar Circus, based in Baraboo, Wisconsin, prompted this return trip in 1909.

Every celebration deserves a parade. C.E. Williams did his part to decorate and drive the float in a Wall Lake Fourth of July parade. The float, pictured around 1910, advertises flour and showcases a woman baking bread. The white-clad passengers did not need to worry about flour showing on their clothing.

Decoration Day (now called Memorial Day) began as a time to honor those who had died in the Civil War. The holiday gradually evolved into a time to honor all who had died by placing flowers on their graves. Parades and public gatherings were commonplace. In 1909, people gathered on Lake View's Main Street to celebrate.

Not all parades are celebrations. Rural communities are noted for caring for neighbors at times of need. When a farmer is hurt, neighbors work to complete planting or harvesting. When someone dies, people gather to support the family, bringing food and sending flowers as memorial tributes. Friends and family follow the funeral coach as the body of a friend and loved one is transported to the cemetery in Odebolt.

Bringing World War I tanks to Sac City was one way to boost sales of war bonds and recruit men to enlist in the military. A soldier talks to a captivated group of onlookers on Sac City's Main Street as the driver demonstrates the tank's maneuverability while peering from the small opening that could be closed to help protect those inside.

"Midway" on Sac County Fair Grounds, Sac City, Iowa.
Photo by Hout.

County residents anxiously awaited the Sac County Fair. Each year, thousands of people gathered to visit with friends, walk the midway, and check out the newest vendors. The opportunity to showcase livestock and produce, while being entertained by gravity-defying daredevils, was a celebration of summer and provided needed energy for the long winter ahead. Sac County's fairgrounds hosted the first fair in 1871. The trio of fliers at right entertained audiences in 1909.

A parade in front of the grandstand at the 1910 Sac County Fair featured members of the clown band in uniform and beautifully decorated automobiles. The octagonal announcer's stand also served as a bandstand for the men's chorus, who serenaded the cars and passengers as they passed by. Advertising spots on the stand were highly coveted and paid for a large portion of the fair costs.

Race Track at Fair Grounds.

Harness races drew huge crowds to the Sac County Fair. Although gambling was illegal in Sac County, there certainly were a few friendly wagers among friends who supported different horses. Sac County had a long tradition of raising fine horses and developing them into winning racers.

A parade often marked the beginning of the county fair. The horse-drawn float with fair royalty makes its way down Sac City's Main Street before the official opening of the 1906 countywide festivities. People took great pride in the ability to transform a wooden farm wagon into a thing of beauty.

AUBURN 40    SAC CITY RACES    RAB.

Automobile racing became a popular attraction at Sac County's fairgrounds. Spectators cheered not only for their favorite drivers, but for their favorite cars. Both the Auburn and Ford cars create a cloud of dust, but only the Auburn carries a passenger, which helps to change the vehicle's center of gravity for the turns. The modified Model T race car reached 107.8 miles per hour on a frozen lake; the Sac County performance was certainly not quite that fast.

FORD RACER    SAC CITY    RW

Sac City Chautauqua, 1906.

After the turn of the 20th century, traveling Chautauqua programs were regular occurrences in many Iowa communities. Sac County was no exception. The two-week programs were great successes. The crowds at the 1906 event in Sac City prompted community leaders to erect a permanent Chautauqua pavilion in 1908 to avoid the discomfort of sitting in a large tent in humid Iowa summers. Chautauqua programs in Odebolt utilized tents from 1912 to 1930.

Sac City Chautauqua, U.S.A.

W.J. Bryan at Sac City Chautauqua.

Traveling Chautauqua programs brought entertainment, education, and political awareness to rural communities. The 1907 Chautauqua in Sac City was held in a large tent and featured famed orator and presidential candidate William Jennings Bryan. The success of this series of programs prompted a group of investors to build the Proudfoot & Bird–designed Chautauqua pavilion as a permanent location for the two-week summer events. The building still stands and is one of the few remaining Chautauqua auditoriums in the United States. Thousands of people from the surrounding area flocked to Sac City to attend; many camped along the riverfront during their stay.

Sac City Chautauqua U.S.A.

The Chautauqua movement originated in Upstate New York as a vehicle to educate Sunday school teachers. The traveling programs retained an educational component and actively empowered women to seek education. People came from the surrounding area to the Sac City event. As World War I dawned, patriotism swept the land. Chautauqua programs were no exception. This 1914 view of the interior of the pavilion demonstrates that one flag is certainly never enough. In 1914, it was not uncommon to display the American flag with the field of stars on the right.

Although Sac County towns frequently worked together, there were certainly times of rivalry. A Fourth of July baseball game between Schaller and Early would have been one of those times. The large crowd attests to the support each community's team enjoyed. Baseball was a popular pastime for young and old.

Picnics and pickup ball games were popular forms of entertainment. Well-dressed revelers gather around Wall Lake (now Black Hawk Lake) to watch and cheer for their favorite athletes. Women took great care to use parasols to protect themselves from the sun.

ODEBOLT, IOWA, FOOTBALL TEAM. 1911.
MILTON. LEFT HALFBACK.

School sporting events have long been popular in Sac County. Football has changed drastically over the past 100 years. Pads and helmets were not part of the sport in 1911. The wooden basketball backboard certainly was not built to withstand someone hanging from the rim after making a dunk.

The Sac City Institute was a church-sponsored college that specialized in training teachers and also boasted a music conservatory. The 1903 football team proudly represented Sac County with a winning season. The team traveled to games by rail and frequently had to stay overnight before returning to Sac City and student life.

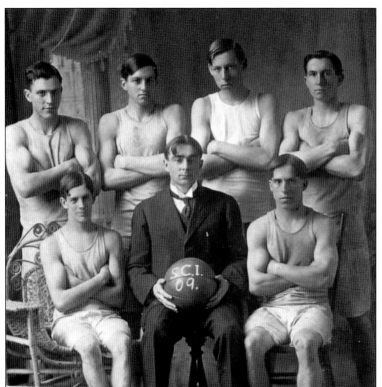

Sac City Institute's basketball team also had to travel by rail to compete with other teams. The 1909 team's six members, shown with their coach, had a very successful undefeated season. The players' pleasure in showcasing biceps could not quite produce any smiles for the photograph.

Physical training was an important part of schools' curriculums. In addition to building strong bodies, athletics helped bolster school spirit and provided entertainment for the community. Track teams were very popular. This 1930s photograph shows a Sac City athlete watching a member of a rival team compete in the long jump in front of a group of well-dressed spectators.

Hunting was a way to feed the family and a source of entertainment for many. Prior to tiling farm ground, Sac County had many acres of swamplands, which were home to waterfowl. The abundant wildlife made the county a popular destination for hunters. The men in this photograph had no shortage of hunting equipment.

Fishing is a great form of recreation as well as a way to put food on the table. These four men had a successful day at Black Hawk Lake in 1916. People traveled for many miles to enjoy the bountiful catches and time on the lake.

Black Hawk Lake in Lake View is the southernmost glacier-formed lake in Iowa. After the turn of the 20th century, trains from Denison and increased usage of the automobile made the lake a popular tourist attraction. Fishing from the dock and rowing a boat were enjoyable activities in the early decades of the century. The need to wash and iron dresses did not hamper the enjoyment of the beautiful lake.

Visitors to Lakewood on Black Hawk Lake in Lake View often arrived by train and then took a ride on the *Eclipse* to cross the lake and arrive at a cottage. Travel in Sac County frequently included land, rail, and water.

The lure of cool water attracted many tourists to Lakewood. Families built small summer homes along the lakeshore. The waterslide was a popular attraction. Bathers rode wood platforms like the ones pictured as they careened from a slide into the lake. Swimming attire has changed significantly since 1910.

A large wooden slide was a popular attraction in the Lakewood area. The climb up the stairs was worth the thrill of soaring down the slide on a wooden float to splash into the lake on a hot and humid Sac County summer day in 1912.

Visitors who did not own a cabin or preferred a few more comforts could stay at the Lakewood Park Hotel. The large open porch offered a shaded outdoor location with a lake view. The hotel offered bleacher seating for people to view the beautiful sailboats that oftentimes sailed on Black Hawk Lake.

Lakewood, near Lake View, was a popular tourist destination on Wall Lake, which is now known as Black Hawk Lake. The name change helped alleviate confusion, as the town of Wall Lake was not by Wall Lake. Boating, fishing, and enjoying the large waterslide inspired visitors to ride the train to Lake View to vacation.

After the Great Depression, jobs were scarce. The Works Progress Administration (WPA) employed many men and provided needed income to help feed their families. The stone shelter house in Sac City's Chautauqua Park was a 1939 WPA construction project. Large local stones and native lumber combined to produce a picturesque shelter with a double fireplace. The building is still in use and is listed in the National Register of Historic Places.

A waterslide is a big attraction, whether into a river or a lake. The riverfront in Sac City was a popular attraction on hot summer days, even though these people from 1910 do not appear to be dressed to go in the water. Community members worked together to develop recreational opportunities and create chances to enjoy the area's natural beauty.

A hot-air balloon draws a crowd in Wall Lake. The first manned balloon flight took place in 1783 in France. Even though the means of transportation was well over 100 years old, a balloon ascent was an unusual event in Sac County in the early 1900s.

In the days before radio and television, gathering around the piano in the parlor was a popular form of family entertainment. For those without piano skills, player pianos, like the one in this 1908 Schaller photograph, allowed anyone to sound like a seasoned virtuoso.

For some, the chance to meet friends and catch up on the latest town news was more entertaining than shopping in this South Sixth Street store in Sac City, which offered fresh peaches for 25¢ a basket, boxes of cornflakes, and Bon Ami cleaner, "tough on grime, simple on ingredients." Business districts served every community as a place to acquire both social interaction and goods.

Refreshments, candy, and even a duckpin bowling alley (using small pins) provide ample enjoyment for young and old. The open stairway led to Sac City's opera house, which had a stage complete with permanent backdrops that helped transport people to a different time and place during stage performances.

P.T. Barnum knew how to promote people. His billing of the world's smallest man helped make Tom Thumb weddings popular pageants in which children acted out a wedding ceremony. Inspired by the 1863 marriage of General Tom Thumb (Charles Stratton) and Lavinia Warren, these two adorable children in Odebolt undoubtedly brought tears and smiles to all who watched the spectacle in 1910.

Most communities have unique celebrations. Early's May fete celebrated the beginning of summer. Some mothers spent a lot of time creating butterfly costumes so these young girls could entertain those celebrating the end of the school year in 1923.

Mock weddings were a fun way for friends and relatives to honor brides-to-be. Several women dressed as men added to the festivities. Those attending this party in Early also dressed their (perhaps reluctant) children for the occasion. It is only fitting to wonder who sold or made children's tuxedos in 1911.

Innovation characterized all forms of entertainment in Sac County. When finances were tight, Hobart Hill used spare pieces of farm equipment to make a fun racer to entertain the neighborhood children. His creativity symbolizes the pioneer spirit that drove residents to build beautiful churches, participate in the performing arts, and find new ways to enjoy the natural beauty of rural Iowa.

*Four*

# BUILDING CONNECTIONS

Transforming a prairie into an attractive place for settlers is a slow process. Building roads and railroads is a costly endeavor. Sac County was laid out in square mile sections with roads around nearly every section. Every river crossing required a bridge. Every road required maintenance.

People worked tirelessly to bring railroads to their communities. Offers of land and money were commonplace events when attracting railroad companies. Once train tracks came to town, there was considerable competition to update depots and increase the frequency of trains.

Cars, motorcycles, bicycles, and horses helped move people from one place to another. Although county rivers are not navigable, there was some boat transportation on Black Hawk Lake.

As transportation improved, the county continued to grow. Visitors saw the county as a land of opportunity and chose to invest. Residents gained easier access to new ideas. Building connections is an endless journey that continues to this day as roads improve, telecommunication capability increases, and people make new friends.

George Simmons and Mabel Hines enjoy a 1912 buggy ride near Sac City. In addition to trains, transportation at the time included horseback riding, horse-drawn wagons, bicycles, and automobiles. Some homes continued to have a small barn to accommodate the horses. As time passed, these barns were often converted into garages for the new automobiles.

A trip to the ice cream parlor on horseback was a fun way to gather with friends. In 1907, a cigar and confections store on North Fifth Street in Sac City was a popular attraction. Hitching posts were scattered throughout town to allow riders to leave their horses in safety while enjoying an ice cream soda.

Railroad access helped build Sac County. The Chicago & Northwestern (C&NW) Depot in Auburn was perhaps the most important building in town. The railroad company platted the town and brought prosperity to the area when the line between Lake City and Wall Lake was completed in 1886. Like most C&NW depots, this one followed the company's stock plans to create an identifiable design.

The Chicago & Northwestern Depot in Odebolt was unusual with its open freight areas on either end. Trains provided passenger service and the ability to transport goods. The raised platform beside the depot provided easy access to train cars. This 1913 view clearly shows the roofline that is atypical of other depots in the area.

The Chicago & Northwestern Depot in Wall Lake was a hub of rail traffic in the county. Passenger trains provided relatively easy access for area residents to travel to any location with rail connections. The depot is listed in the National Register of Historic Places and currently is a museum.

Grain elevators and railroad tracks are natural partners. This 1910 postcard shows Schaller's depot in the distance and four large grain storage facilities. Having a nearby elevator to sell grain was a huge advantage for farmers in an era before large grain transport was commonplace.

Before railroad access, farmers struggled to sell crops and livestock. When railroads opened a new line, an old railcar oftentimes served as the first depot. Small-town depots frequently had a second story for the stationmaster's living quarters. The 1899 Milwaukee Railroad depot in Lytton had areas for passengers (on the left) and freight (on the right). When the depot was constructed, the town of Lytton was nearly nonexistent. The depot in Nemaha had a similar design and also sparked growth of the community.

Since engineers prided themselves on punctuality, waiting for the train to arrive was a predictable experience. The station agent made sure freight was unloaded quickly and passengers were safely on board so the train could be promptly on its way to the next destination, as evidenced by the people prepared to greet the Chicago & Northwestern train at the Early depot.

Transporting grain with horse-drawn wagons was slow at best, so having depots relatively close to farms was a driving factor in community development. The depot in Early appears to be part of a grain elevator complex in this 1910 photograph. Railcars could be loaded directly from the grain storage, creating an easy and efficient way to market bountiful crops.

Sac City's Chicago & Northwestern Depot was constructed in 1916 to replace the earlier wood-frame depot, pictured above. Built as a combination freight-and-passenger depot, the building followed the company's No. 1 Plan, which was used for many midsized communities. Men's and women's waiting rooms were on either side of the conductor's station; freight-loading facilities were on the left side of the building.

Railroad service was a vital link that connected communities to the world. The Chicago, Milwaukee & St. Paul was one of two lines in Sac City to provide passenger service and help bring lumber, livestock, and other goods to the area. The nearby Park Hotel provided shuttle service to assist salespeople with sharing their goods and expertise with local residents.

Railroad access and hotel accommodations are vital for community growth. This early-1900s photograph clearly shows the proximity of both in Wall Lake. After coming to Wall Lake as a partner in the creamery, Dan Brunton built this hotel in 1900. It was a popular destination for traveling salesmen and termed the best hotel between Carroll and Sioux City.

The sprawling hotel in Odebolt welcomed visitors into a homelike environment. The spacious screened porch was an ideal space to enjoy a cool summer breeze and escape flies and mosquitos. The L-shaped layout was a creative solution to building a hotel on a corner lot.

The Hotel Park in Sac City was considered the finest lodging facility between Fort Dodge and Sioux City. Built in 1912 and enlarged in 1917, the hotel and restaurant offered fine accommodations for traveling salesmen. The original part abutted an older wood-frame hotel. Brisk business necessitated tearing down the older structure and expanding the hotel to the south. The favorable location near Highway 20 and two passenger train depots helped business prosper. The hotel offered 50 guest rooms, sample rooms for salesmen to showcase goods, a lobby with Art Deco tiled floors, and several apartments. The D.M. Farmer family owned and operated the hotel for many years. The building still stands and is listed in the National Register of Historic Places.

As people began traveling cross-country in automobiles, tourist parks opened in many communities. Camping was an affordable way for families to spend the night while on the road. The tourist park behind Sac City's Chautauqua pavilion offered cooking facilities, the opportunity to fish for dinner, and shaded comfort for hot days.

Trains, like automobiles, were subject to accidents. When a car jumped the tracks or a bridge failed, the damage could be severe. The railroad companies had special cranes on railcars to assist in repairing damages when accidents like this happened. This passenger car was stranded on a bridge near Sac City.

Building a metal bridge in Iowa winter conditions had to have been a miserable job. Pictured around 1914, workmen are seen constructing a bridge over the North Raccoon River. Using a carefully rigged pully system, they are placing the iron support system above the substructure made of wood. Bridges in rural areas could save miles of travel.

Bridge building was hard work that required careful oversight to assure quality and safety. Without bridges, transportation would be, at best, challenging. In 1911, a new bridge spanned the North Raccoon River in Sac City. Increasing numbers of automobiles in the county required stronger and more stable bridges.

Bridges connect communities. Although many bridges span bodies of water, the Ninth Street Bridge in Sac City allowed traffic to pass over the ravine that transects the town. This 1911 postcard shows seven men and a well-dressed overseer constructing a bridge that helped the town grow and open up new housing areas in the southern part of the community. The 1912 view shows the completed bridge with the Sac City Institute buildings in the background.

A county's commitment to education speaks volumes about the citizens' desire to spark growth. Country schools allowed many younger students ready access to education; transportation to high school proved more difficult for some rural residents. This 1915 horse-drawn private school bus in Nemaha allowed rural students the opportunity to complete high school and travel in relative comfort.

Jimmy Ward's 1910 flight into Sac City was the first airplane landing in the area. The open biplane landed at the fairgrounds. There has never been a commercial airport in Sac County. Sac City does have a municipal airport, and there are several private landing strips in the county.

Boats were a huge attraction on Black Hawk Lake. Sailboats, steamboats, and a paddleboat transported people from one side of the lake to the other and allowed tourists who did not have a boat to enjoy time on the water. The dock was obviously not used for fishing. The sign reminds people that "fishing from this dock is strictly prohibited."

The choice between Indian motorcycles and Harley Davidson motorcycles was frequently a cause for great debate. A friendly race was one way to settle the debate about which was better. These two gentlemen are more than ready to demonstrate which brand could perform better in a 1930s race at Sac County's fairgrounds. The Harley is on the left, and the Indian is on the right.

Motorcycles were not limited to racing. From 1907 to 1915, the US Postal Service allowed rural carriers to deliver mail from motorcycles. Some used sidecars to help with larger volumes of mail. S.R. Bodwell demonstrates the ease of delivery from his Indian motorcycle, which was probably purchased at Strohmeir's store in Sac City.

Jan 26 '06 Dear Brother and Wife - We two

The transition from horse-drawn transportation to motor vehicles changed the face of Sac County. Improved ability to travel from one area to another allowed for better communications. The advent of the automobile brought the need for better roads. Ben Buehler's car, with a crank start and right-hand steering, was a fun way for two dapper gentlemen to travel in 1906.

Sac County residents loved automobiles. In fact, they had more per capita than any other area of Iowa. The steering wheel on the right side of the car, ornate headlights, and a horn that just begs to be squeezed make this open touring car a perfect match for the well-dressed passengers. The canvas cover proudly bearing "Sac City" leaves no doubt where these people called home.

The 1920s Lincoln was a sturdy automobile. Even when flipped at a high rate of speed, the damage was relatively minimal. Broken glass and some scratches on the top were the extent of damages in this 1926 single-car accident near Odebolt. Everyone escaped without injury.

Travel, like building communities, is not without perils. Early automobile tires were prone to flats. Many cars came equipped with a hand-powered tire pump and tire patches for on-the-road repairs. The women travelers from Sac City appear more than slightly displeased at the interruption in their scheduled trip. The ingenuity these passengers used to tackle their problems is a fitting image of Sac County residents' ability to meet problems, solve them, and transform the prairie into a vibrant group of communities.

# BIBLIOGRAPHY

Auburn Centennial Book Committee. *Auburn: 1887–1987.* Self-published, 1987.

Brewer, Zaidee, et al. *Early, Iowa: 1882–1982.* Odebolt, IA: The Odebolt Chronicle Print, 1982.

Denise, Theodore. *The History of Lytton, Iowa.* Rockwell City, IA: *Calhoun County Reminder,* 1982.

Hart, William H. *History of Sac County, Iowa.* Indianapolis, IN: B.F. Bowen & Company, Inc., 1914.

Hogue, Jean. *Schaller, Iowa: 1883–1983.* Self-published, 1983.

Host, Sandra Kessler. *Adams Ranch Story.* Omaha, NE: Standard Printing Co., 2019.

Hunter, Ken, and Arline Hunter, eds. *Lake View: 1880–1980.* Odebolt, IA: The Odebolt Chronicle Print, 1980.

Peterson, Eleanor, ed. *As Time Goes By: Odebolt Centennial.* Odebolt, IA: The Odebolt Chronicle Print, 1977.

Phillips, Shirley, et al. *Reflections: Sac City Quasquicentennial, 1855–1980.* Odebolt, IA: The Odebolt Chronicle Print, 1980.

———. *Sac City, Iowa Established 1855.* N.p., n.p., 2005.

Waters, Marlys, ed. *Nemaha, Iowa Centennial Book: Nemaha Town History 1899–1999.* CA: CreateSpace Publishing, 1999.

Wilhoite, Lee, et al. *A Century of Living in Wall Lake: 1877–1977.* Self-published, 1977.

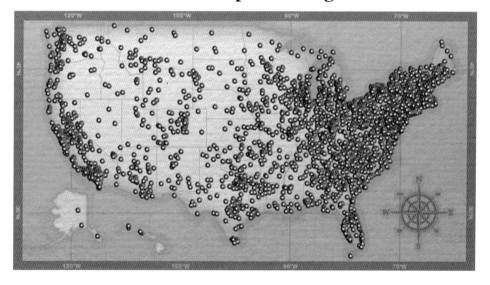